Rain
& Other
Mellow
Things

Nisha Singh

authorHOUSE°

AuthorHouse™
1663 Liberty Drive
Bloomington, IN 47403
www.authorhouse.com
Phone: 1 (800) 839-8640

Published by AuthorHouse 06/15/2016

ISBN: 978-1-5246-1402-7 (sc)
ISBN: 978-1-5246-1401-0 (e)

Library of Congress Control Number: 2016909711

Print information available on the last page.

To my mom.

A woman who has survived the most colossal
of battles and continues to find happiness in
the little ones she's faced with every day.

To my dad.

A man who finds laughter in everything,
and has persistence like no other.

Thank you for everything before, now, and in advance.

I love you both more than you can imagine.

A small yet frank note.

Dear reader,

Thank you for accepting this gift. From me to you. A complete exposition of myself in words. I can tell you with a stretched smile and beaming eyes that writing this book and the journey of what it has become has truly made me happy. These poems and pieces of prose bound together before you range from simple thoughts to perceptions of human nature, to the depth of culture and social justice. It is my deepest wish that you enjoy what lies before you. From feminist poetry to the inquiry of the heart. My world, at this moment, plainly lies in your hands. I ask you to handle it with care, and urge you to find parts of yourself in these pages.

Live and love as if walls don't exist.

With sincerity,

Nisha Singh

Contents

Chapter I

Justice and Something Sweeter.

A chapter dedicated to strife and strength of the minority.

The pain
Of things of that magnitude
Is too powerful,
To be conveniently packaged
Into neat little letters.
Too agonizing,
To be punctuated,
Into little paused phrases.
Black ink,
On white paper,
Will never show blood.
—*newspapers*

My women are sleeved in dusk
And carry stories deeper than the seas on their backs.
My women have eyes dark as night
And skin as thick as the bark of trees.
My women are not given enough respect for their labor,
And are constantly told they are worth less or not at all.
My women are shamed for looking the way they do,
Yet cannot alter themselves to look *too* beautiful without being
humiliated.
My women's history is shoved away,
Behind books and shelves where dust meets.
My women are idolized as virgins
And when lost, thrown like carcasses onto a road.
My women are seen as items to be bought,
A father having to pay another when his daughter is wed.
My women are harassed,
For simply being.
My women
Are not given
Enough credit
For the strength
And endurance
They possess.
Continuing to live
Despite all of this
And more.
—औरत

I will never understand
Humans' need
For dominance.
Some desire people have
To deprive others of their
Culture.
Color.
Home.
How do we have the courage
To continue to glorify
Something so
Vile?
Why create
A scheme
Where nobody wins
And everybody
Inevitably loses?
We are all people.
We begin
And end the same.
Who's to change that?
—centuries and still no one knows

And yet
You believe
That you have the authority
To tell me
What will be offensive,
And what will be acceptable.
All the while
You don't realize
How that is oppression
In and of itself.
—*easy to say what is painful and what is comical when it doesn't concern your people*

Not a word of English
Escapes from their lips
Yet the lines on their faces
Speak stories louder than any
Documents tell.
And yet the world dreads them
Rather than appreciating their toil.
Their struggle.
Their pain.
It must be so easy
To spew hatred
Against those
Who make it possible
For a nation to breathe.
—*greencards, tears, and hope*

They see burned buildings.
I see a mother's anguish.
They see criminals.
I see frustration.
They do not realize
No one would run
If streets didn't mean
Such misfortune.
They see a nationwide case.
I see human betrayal.
"Can you blame him?"
"I can blame what he was taught."
—*2014 before and after*

Tell me
Grounds are equal
When you are in my position.
Live the lives
Of these children,
And then tell me
That everyone
Has a chance.
There is simply
No pathway
For success
When your books are filled with lies
And your dreams seem
like silly fantasies.
And shame on me
For being born
And raised
In the wrong neighborhood!
—*across the street*

How must
It feel
To have someone
Miles and miles
Away
Determine
The legitimacy
And validity
Of your love?
How relieving
It must have felt
When they realized
Love
Is exactly the same
No matter
The gender
Or sex.
—*June 26, 2015*

I hope
They realize
When they compliment
The foreign rugs and pashmina scarves
That not only
Paper values
Were paid
But also bloody,
Nimble fingers
And childhoods.
Fingers allowed
Needles to keep
Wounding
Because they were convinced
Their toil
Would result in
Maybe a book
Or a ripe fruit.
—*nasim, an orphan, Pakistan 2013*

Tears stream down
Her olive cheeks
As she fingers
The golden string around her neck.
She does not belong to any country.
She is a foreigner.
Everywhere.
An accent too thick to be "exotic",
And a betrayal too deep to be forgiven.
Hopeless days
And seemingly endless
Black nights.
She hopes that
Her drudgery
Will one day
Mean great things for
And from her children.
—*no, I'm from…*

Woman.
Useless.
Weak.
Woman.
Vagina.
Uterus.
Nothing more.
Nothing less.
Not a human.
No heart.
No brain.
No soul.
Just a body.
Not for herself, however.
For someone else, she is a toy.
Yet we never see
Her godlike patience,
Wisdom beyond time
And strength more powerful than any machine.
Why must we overlook
The control a woman possesses
By merely living?
—*I swear she could leave an ocean barren with one twitch of an eye*

It's incredible
How a population
Is capable of
Constantly dividing within itself.
Furthering hatred
When they all possess
One beating heart,
Hot cerise blood.
They are the same,
But are obsessed with the idea
Of superiority
Inferiority
And selfishness.
Greed
Is not individual to one
Race
Sex
Gender
Or sexuality,
And neither is love.
—*the savage and the king looked the same on their deathbeds,
because even jewels cannot hide what is just purely human.*

I am so much more
Than what they show of my people.
That's when I started to hate silver screens
And the sound of my people's voice.
—*thank you for making my people seem lesser because they don't*
speak the same way you do

She is adorned
With strings of jade
And called beautiful.
But she is never told
Of her worth beyond
The gold on her neck,
The dark lines on her eyes.
She is told
That she is a canvas meant
To be scrawled upon
With untouched silence.
—*the wedding*

Feminism is the movement
For a voice
That is not silenced
And is not afraid to screech.

We live
In a society
Where our worth
Is what we look like
And not what we can make.
—*a hierarchy based on things that have no prospect of change*

Tassels of grass as dark as night
Litter her body.
Magnificent ringlets
A blackish-brown commotion
Rests upon her head like a crown.
Rich olive paints her skin
Paired with warm chocolate eyes like hued morning dew
Speckles of blemished flowers across vast stretches of land.
She is a garden.
But she is taught that she is made of weeds
To be plucked.
Waxed.
Straightened.
Draped.
Lightened.
Why does she long to change to a garden
Of light, silky blades of grass
Azure eyes
Small waists with little to no blossoms,
When both gardens yield from the same soil?
The shame of color,
Is not inbred,
It is instilled.
—*Women of color*

Enjoy the knowledge
I can offer.
Revel in the perspective
I can provide.
Understand that I am no threat.
The more you take me in,
The more the world shall be yours.
—*a note to ignorance*

It's strange
When you somehow
Make a spectacle of yourself
By just being yourself?
—*minority*

From birth
We are taught to believe
There is some void in us
That must be filled
Or some imperfection
That must be corrected
For us to truly be at peace with ourselves.
It is almost revolting
How we don't realize
How ghastly such a thing is
Till a frail teenage girl
Is found alone
In a public bathroom
Vomiting
And a boy
Who doesn't feel like one
Is imprisoned in his own mind
And continues to lie to himself
And others around him
So he can keep
Someone happy.
—*today and sadly tomorrow and quite possibly forever*

If you can walk on two legs
If you can hold your partner's hand in public
If you can run your fingers through your hair
If you can maintain tranquility in your mind
If you don't waver over dollar signs
If you don't feel it is best to stay quiet when men are squawking
If protective measures are made specifically for you and people like you
If you don't turn around whenever you enter your place of worship
If you don't know the whispers like hissing fire in your ears
You have a power.
A limitless power that you use unconsciously,
But can also use for good.
—*privilege shouldn't be a fire that you spit just because you can*

A person's actions are not only
Accountable to them
But also to the man who said
Their homes would get better if they stole.
—*maybe they wouldn't be criminals if they didn't have to*

You are told
Since birth
That you were meant
To fit inside a box.
You were given
Two options.
How does
One proceed
When one feels
Misplaced
In either one
Or recognizes that
They belong in the other?
—*why do we need boxes anyways*

It is amusing to me
How something
I was raised to respect and honor
Is another boy's reason to taunt and slur.
It is amusing to me
How something
I'd consider the true representation of my faith
Makes some tremble with fear.
It is amusing to me
How something
That always made me feel safe
And at home
Is another man's shooting target.
—*the turban: the story of a symbol of safety turned into an*
attraction for racists

The answer
Is not to turn the oppressor's finger
Towards the other community
But rather
To enlighten the oppressor
That there is no reason,
Other than ignorance,
Or a false sense of security,
To lift fingers at all.
—*an unwanted and disgusting question: why don't you just tell people you aren't muslim?*

Ugly truths
Hidden under hurried coats of paint
And artificial promises.
Proud and diverse,
Yet built on the backs of
Exploitation and superiority.
But it is still beautiful.
And I will still love it.
—*difficulties in patriotism and blinded by color*

You deserve so much more
Than what the world dictates for you,
Yet you continue to ask yourself
If the endless condemnation is worth
Equality.
—*she's a bitch because she wants to be seen the way her mother
sees you*

How do you suppose
It feels
When you can't assume safety
Around the ones there to protect
And the ones made to love?
Through no fault but of merely living,
Your world is sideways
And your view seems like a disarray of tears and colors.
Hypocrisy is subtle.
One moment you are told to express and the other
To suppress.
—*thank you for your unnecessary opinion!*

The world would be a better place
If we stopped labelling people
And designating their place
Based on things they cannot control.
The world would be a better place
If our minds were revered as much as
Pieces of paper were.
The world would be a better place
If everybody stopped obsessing
Over some vague perception
Of supremacy,
And just listened.
—*sometimes closing your mouth is the noblest thing you can do*

Chapter II

A Pause for Paragraphs.

A chapter dedicated to the more wordy
and wholesome of pieces.

☼ ☼ ☼

Racial Intolerance in the United States of America

☼ ☼ ☼

☼ ☼ ☼

The hypocrisy of the human mind is outstanding at times. I wonder if our brains were made so that we don't see injustice unless it affects us. I have walked in circles around the same few shops in this mall, and the policeman has continued to diligently follow, his eyes leering at my every movement. And of course, the same thought, the same disgusting and terrible thought runs across my mind. *It's my hair, my skin, my clothes, it's just me.* And this is when I feel trapped inside my body. This is when I feel shame and embarrassment. This is when I begin to resent myself entirely. And this is also when I become infuriated. This is when I will think about how my culture is lionized in media. This is when I will frustrate and confuse myself, thinking: *you love my culture but you fear my people.*

And this is when I will feel like an outsider in my own skin, hair, clothes, and country.

—*ask any person of color, this feeling is as ordinary as laughter*

A young man. Perhaps my son's age. Twenty years in ruins.

GO BACK TO YOUR COUNTRY.

Brilliant red paint. Some of it trickled below the letters that sprawled across the window. Reminiscent of blood. If only this young man, the future of the country that has given me so much, would look beyond the turban that crowns my head. If only he would look beyond the thick beard and mustache. If only he would understand the fear of a father, a husband. A man whose home was lit on fire because he was Sikh. In his very own India. If only he could understand the pain of a seeker of asylum. The pain of fleeing the striking rays of an Indian sun. Rays that turned from warmth to fire. If only he could understand that all I ever prayed for, worked for, was that my son never felt such burns. I attempt to pick up my feet and examine the ruin. My legs weigh too much. The ground drags me down. A sliver of glass catches my eye. I lift it from the cold, gray concrete. As I finger the sharp edges, tears start to form in the corners of my eyes. I see a reflection of the flames.

Another betrayal.

From yet another home.

—*a Sikh man, 2002*

"She doesn't even speak English."

They think I am stupid because I have no means of communication. They are foolish to assume so. I possess a level of intelligence they will never understand. I have seen brothers deprive each other of breath. I have felt the cool, familiar metal of a knife in my back. I have seen destruction. A war of ideals turned into shards of concrete and piles of dust. Worthless stacks of paper.

They look at me, and see an empty human. With a ragged suitcase. A funny accent. The smell of dirt. They even have the audacity to accuse me of entering their country without permission. How can they utter such words, accuse me of being so desperate to leave my beautiful country. How can they charge me with desiring to be slurred at, pointed at, and constantly questioned? How can they fault me, when the already existing guilt inside me adds tons to every step I make in this country?

I am selfish, and now I am a miscreant.

They will give me a roof. They will give me food. They will give me work.

And respect is patiently earned.

Welcome to America.

—*ask any forced immigrant, the feeling becomes smaller and smaller but never leaves*

Do not invalidate my pain by making it a trend. To you, it is a statement. To me, it is my shame. A shame that I will never be rid of simply because it is dried onto my skin.

—*cultural appropriation*

"If you are neutral in situations of injustice, you
have chosen the side of the oppressor."

-Desmond Tutu

Racial intolerance and the institutionalized prejudice
that has dictated the culture and societal pillars of the
United States has affected generations of hard-working
humans. Whether this be your country or not, earning
respect in a society that systematically works against entire
races of people cannot be justified. If you are a witness to
oppression, speak. Words are the most powerful weapon
against the evils that continue to paralyze human rights
progress in a nation I am proud to call my home.

Tell.

A somewhat true tale taking place not too far away

2015

A little boy.

Ahmad.

His family: a mother and father.

His sister, once a newly married, joyful bride.

He now stands in a line.

His once soft, pink hand is now draped in cuts and blisters.

It envelopes his father's bruised pinky.

A small stone, caked with dust and gunpowder, fills the latter of Ahmad's hands.

He names the stone *Habib*, meaning "friend" in his mother tongue, Arabic.

"Marhaban."

He is now in Jordan.

He, his mother, and father are assigned to a tent with two other families. The Hassan and the Amaris.

Ahmad wraps himself in his sister's blue shawl. He takes a deep lungful.

Jasmine.

The moment he recognizes the sweet scent, his eyes fill up with tears.

A sliver of dark gray catches his eye underneath his mother's blanket.

Another small stone.

It's rough.

Patches shield the solid interior.

He proceeds to name the newly discovered stone Aaliyah,

His sister's name.

He places *Habib* next to Aaliyah

And realizes
The Syrian stone
The Jordanian stone
Both blown up
Thrown across
Carved into
In different circumstances.
But to his wallowing
Big
Innocent
Brown eyes
They look
And feel
Exactly the same.
"If only we all perceived humankind like so."

Stamps and rape

I'd heard about people who survived.
Newspapers and stories.
Triumphant comebacks
And a world that smiled in their bravery.
They never show how people change around you.
How everyone seems to throw apologetic looks,
Whispering about the boy who got raped.
Some people were confused as to how it could be.
I couldn't be happy anymore.
I couldn't have dreams.
I didn't want to be the weak boy who lost something
And yet I was told I was the deceitful boy who lied.

I didn't even feel sad.
I was angry.
I was angry at the man who did this to me.
Who got some forgettable joy from a night that would
Last in my mind forever.
I hated flowers.
I would stomp on them.
Crushing every petal slowly.
I believed it to be a perfect representation
Of what would happen to the boy
Who once had everything
And within seconds had nothing.

And the sun rose and died again and again.
The world did not change.
Yet I saw everything differently.
The man is suffering for what he did.
And yet I never felt it help me.

He impressed his fingerprint
Where I did not ask to be stamped.
And while he left,
And the ink was still wet
I realized that I would carry a demonic part of him.
Forever.
And as much as I'd like to wash it off,
It will never really fade.
And that is what devours me.

Violet Skies and Wet Eyes

The door slams behind me,
And the noise
Makes the hairs on the back of my neck
Stand straight up,
As if awakened by some impending danger.
My cheek is still hot.
A faint whisper coddles my red ears,
At least he isn't here anymore.

I woke up twice.
One time at 2:39am.
The next at 4:28am.
My body felt like it had been engulfed in icy water,
But my neck felt like burning stove.
His shoes are still at the door.
The bruise is a dark red.
Are you okay? What's that on your cheek?
I just fell on the stairs, nothing to worry about.

The doorbell rang.
And I quickly grabbed a knife.
I slowly opened the door.
He came back.
With roses and an apologetic grin.
I promise I'll change.
You said that the last time.
Well, you aren't some saint. You push me to that point.

And it happened again.
It wasn't a palm this time though.
It was a fist.
My eye was swollen.
It hurt to cry.
I woke up again too.
This time at 1:15am and 3:54am.
You've been coming in with bruises a lot. Is everything okay?
Her shirt was soaking in tears within ten minutes.

He found me.
Even at this woman's apartment.
Does he love pain that much?
He rapped the door furiously, and I started shaking.
She shoved me into a coat closet, and opened the door before he did.
I heard a scream.
And the shattering of glass.
And then sirens.

"Don't stay outside too long! You'll get darker!"
"It's very hard to find boys for dark skinned girls."

"She spent the entire summer in the pool, no wonder she looks like she rolled around in the mud."

"You know, I've been trying some of those lightening creams, and they're really working! I've been getting more compliments, ha!"

"She's a gorgeous, fair-skinned girl. Also educated."

"Yeah, I've been scrubbing my skin with these exfoliating beads, and it's left some rashes."

"Stay in the shade, you're dark enough."

From when we were children, we were convinced that our color was something to be ashamed of. A mistake. We learned that our color was unnatural. Ugly. Our color by itself repelled men. We were taught that whiteness was a standard, and anything else was something we ought to scrub off. We denied our color, told ourselves that God didn't make us like this on purpose. We understood that we could never really see ourselves as beautiful, because there would always be another woman who was lighter. Better. Our mothers and grandmothers and sisters tried to protect us. But the stigma of darkness had become our culture, and their pain became our pain. A culture where we hated ourselves and praised women who didn't even look like us. Women who we could never be.

Do not tell any of my sisters of color
to change their appearance.

They have tried.

We have tried.

Our stories are too incredible to be weakened.

—*colorism: a culture and the fantasy*

He whispered three simple words into her left ear that she will never forget as long as she lives on this warm green earth. Three words so neat yet so vague like a stroke of dazzling violet paint on an empty white screen. Saddening but their intended significance may never be deciphered until we recover the creator of the spoken word herself. The words fell into her skull, embedded their colors into her childish mind, and seeped through the tears that fled her eyes as she watched him walk away without the slightest of emotion.

Maybe that is the effect of hope on humans. It makes us skeptics, yet it helps us breathe. Hope is the sweetest of poisons that we are fed the moment we are released from our mothers' wombs. Hope is dangerous. But we are selfish and continue to feed ourselves with something that continues to weaken us. Because we would rather pleasure ourselves with daydreams than accept life as it comes. Bitter.

—*in another life*

Chapter III

Intricacies of the Human Mind.

A chapter dedicated to the vulnerability of the human heart and the passion of the human thought.

And two paths.
A heart's desire
And a mind's order.
Human and confused,
You stand.
Even bones will hinder your innocence
And remind you,
"Be watchful young traveler,
I was once living too."
—*train tracks, sidewalks, and decisions*

And you will come home.
Maybe guilty.
Maybe sad.
Maybe even satisfied with yourself.
You'll get up the next morning,
And you'll breathe the same way.
But me?
Your eyes will look different.
I won't have the courage to look into them again.
But me?
Your laughter will make my stomach sink.
I will try to plug my ears with some song you used to hate.
But me?
The perfume you'll reek of at 3am will make tears stream from
my eyes.
Almost like a river.
But me?
You will come home.
But I will never feel home again.
—*I'm sorry I ever made you feel this way*

It's almost laughable
How small
You can make someone feel
When only a mere
Few seconds ago
You made them feel
Like they
Owned this world.
—*twists and turns*

When do we lose childhood?
And learn of adulthood?
How confusing it is
For us to understand
Where we fit
In a society that constantly
Reprimands us to grow up,
When only moments ago
We are told to remain with a level of
Innocence.
—*menstruation doesn't determine womanhood because it is a state of mind*

It's too bad
We can't hear
The whispers and murmurs
Inside others' minds.
We mistake simplicity
For stupidity,
And happiness
For peace.
We can never really know.
Smiles can hide
Storms.
Tears can hide
Will.
—*try and you never know what you'll find*

Everything we insist
On holding onto
Is some sort of shame,
And I don't know
How to change,
Or who to blame.
—*your mind, others' words*

Tell me your stories
And open my eyes.
Full moons
And lives that run around papers.
Surely there's something more
We reach for
And your story
Would make finding what I think I've lost
Less strange for me understand.
—*maybe it's because you can't even imagine*

What would you say?
What would you do?
If the clouds we stared at fell apart
And laughter turned into shrieking?
If roses turned sour
And the stories that you convinced
Yourself were true
Were all a game?
Would you stay?
Even lions
Fear the shot
Of a gun
And even humans fear
Emotion.
—*flowers and feelings*

I change too often
For someone
To accept my past,
Enjoy my present,
And eagerly await my future.
—*messes are creative at least*

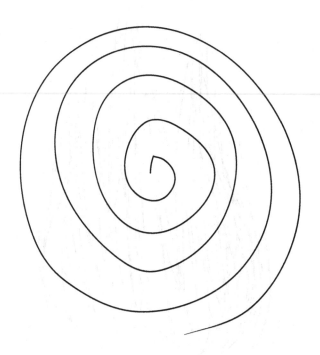

How can one be frightened
When one has seen the pits of hell
And laughed?
—*what is fear to a puppet?*

I submerge myself
Into waters that do not invite me.
They do not keep me afloat.
I drown into an unknown abyss.
Falling deeper and deeper
Where sunlight doesn't touch.
Yet a grin stretches across my tired face.
I am free of sin.
I have been cleansed.
Could I be loved again?
Am I as pure as you desire me?
Have my flaws simply
Been lifted off my skin
And soul?
My home doesn't let me breathe,
And that is why I am blessed.
—*is this the pain they talked about?*

And their smile was
Something I couldn't explain.
It made me feel yellow.
I don't know if it was heaven,
And maybe it was their innocence
That I longed for.
But love is inevitable,
And admiration is matchless.
—*but why did their gender matter!*

Sweeter than roses,
And yet it leaves
My knees scraped.
Do divine things
Hurt this much?
You indulge
But you never prosper.
Because you're hypnotized?
You believed in happiness
And were fooled.
—*Brooklyn dreams and coffee tears*

You block
The only air I can breathe
And force me to live.
Maybe it is the pain
That I am afraid of.
Something greater lurks
And I may never know
What lies beyond?
The fence you built for me.
The hands that once
Held softly
Can now be found
Around my neck.
And I smile weakly.
"At least I am safe."
—*she does her best to please*

It's the laughter
That I miss the most.
And what brings me to tears
Is the fact I will never hear it
Again.
The simplest things
Can liven humans
And we waste our time
With plastic boxes
And gold.
—*may 16, 2015*

It's the questions I've passed.
The unknown is sometimes so painful,
But there's a superiority in staying quiet
For others.
—*high roads that we are blind to*

Part of living
Is fear.
Just because you aren't upset
With seeing life
In black and white
Doesn't mean you are content.
Perhaps you'll fall in love
With pink?
"Why do we keep searching?"
"Because humans are ungrateful, and have an innate need to
search for a new lens, which leads to their own downfall."
"Or maybe bliss?"
—*roofs and cans*

Ask yourself what value you possess
Before looking beneath your wide nose
And smirking.
Do not revere yourself so much.
Your ship is still at sea,
And who knows whose hand is guiding it.
—*hypocrisy*

As the machinery begins to whir,
He looks through the steel bars
And takes one last glance.
Will fruit taste the same?
Will laughter feel the same?
Will he be the same?
The ground beneath his feet
Begins to travel.
He commands himself
To look forward.
The option to return
Is always present.
But a small,
Almost irrelevant,
Part of his mind
Irks him to think otherwise.
"You can only stand witness to change, can't you?"
—*leaving*

The most stunning
The most beautiful
And the most brilliant
Because when you first see it
It seems shoddy and overdone
But when you experience it
You feel so infinitesimally small
Yet you are able to converse
With the moon and sun themselves
Like its buildings and dreams.
—*new york city*

As her tongue turned the brightest blue,
She witnessed the saddest of all farewells.
Sidewalks were not safe anymore,
And moons were not crescents.
The only thing that kept her on earth
Was snatched from her small hands
In a matter of seconds.
—*thoughts*

You think
People cannot see beyond
The gossamer beads of water
That travel down your cheek.
I know for a fact
They are sweeter than honey.
You think
People cannot see beyond
Your pleas for acceptance.
I know for a fact
The ink is borrowed.
You think
People cannot see beyond
Your quaking hands.
And how lonely it must feel,
To stand where no one else has stood.
—*you are entirely fabricated*

How much must she love
Those small fingers,
That she is willing
To jump in fires,
Drown in tears,
Face absolute
Ostracization,
So that those fingers
Never feel
Pain.
—*mother*

Before your light touched my eyes,
My back was adorned with the weight of the entire world.
And I never knew how light and sugary air could taste like.
You made me realize
That no amount of honors or people could make me feel anything.
All I needed was to see myself,
And smile for once.
—*i was born with everything I'd ever needed and nobody said anything*

Drenching yourself
In the pity
You feed yourself
Will never lead you
To the happiness you long for.
You will sink in the grave
You continue to dig for yourself.
Stand up
Rinse the dirt from underneath your knees
Realize
Life has given you much more
Than you can understand
Live and love
For those who cannot.
—*the self-made miser*

You look at me
And stars don't shine.
They stare into my eyes
And sing me songs of
Safety
And persuade me to trust.
They were so beautiful
I'd fall into anyone who beckoned.
A euphoria that created strength
But also made me weak.
It felt like a petal and smelled sweet
Yet it pierced into thick skin.
And that is why it's dismissed.
Because it is peculiar.
Strange.
And perhaps an infatuation
That is mistaken for passion.
And we are left wishing for it
At times we call
"Right".
—*young and "in love"?*

Life is like smoke
After blowing out a candle.
You never know
How fast time flies
And where it goes.
But,
It was worth being there
To watch.
To know
That you were there to
Observe how delicate
And beautiful
It was,
And also
Understand the solemn fact
That you might not remember it.
—*a continuation of thoughts*

Imagination is only prized while it is productive
And is stupid when it is unrealistic.
When do we start to pity
A hopeless daydreamer?
—*feels like we only go backwards*

I don't even know what is real
And I don't even know what I choose to believe.
Why isn't ignorance an easier choice,
And why isn't convenience a dream?
—*wanting too much is a curse and a blessing*

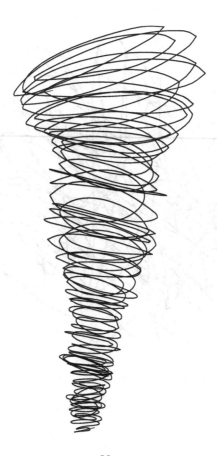

I wish
That my mind
Didn't wander as much.
—*there are oceans in my tears and hurricanes in my mind but all anybody sees is a person*